Painting Miniature Military Figures

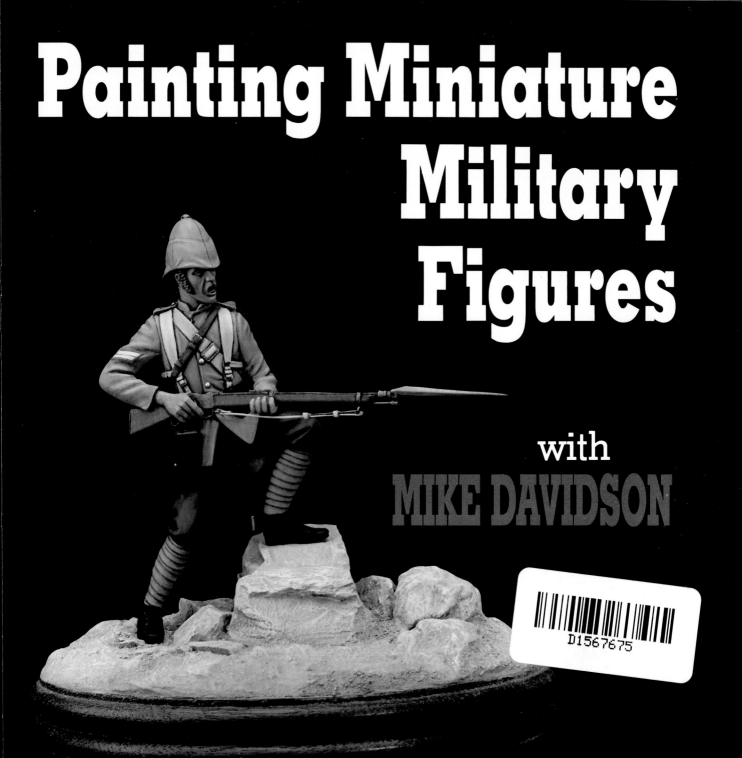

with

MIKE DAVIDSON

77 Lower Valley Road, Atglen, PA 19310

Text written with
& photography by
Douglas Congdon-Martin

ACKNOWLEDGEMENTS

I would like to thank Mike Stelzel and Jon Maguire for their help in producing this effort.

DEDICATION

To my wife, Susan, and my parents, Bill and Jean Davidson, for their support and encouragement.

CONTENTS

Copyright © 1994 by Mike Davidson
Library of Congress Catalog Number: 94-66368

Printed in China
ISBN: 0-88740-625-4

We are interested in hearing from authors with book ideas on related topics.

Published by Schiffer Publishing Ltd.
77 Lower Valley Road
Atglen, PA 19310
Please write for a free catalog. This book may be purchased from the publisher. Please include $2.95 postage.
Try your bookstore first.

INTRODUCTION

The painting of miniature soldiers is not a new hobby. The Pharaohs were entombed with painted miniature soldiers to guard their king in the afterlife. Since then, people of all ages have spent many hours painting soldiers, whether as a pasttime or as a commercial endeavor.

This book will introduce the hobbyist to the basics of painting commercial castings of military miniatures. Also known as connoiseur figures to distinguish them from toy soldiers, the style of painting sets them apart from their toy soldier brethren. They have a more realistic finish as opposed to the accurate but glossy finish applied to toy soldiers.

The variety of these figures available today is almost limitless. No matter what size figure the painter prefers to paint, the selection of historical time period and nationality is great. While the vast majority of figures are of military subjects, many non-military figures are also produced. Figures from the American West, the Victorian period, and famous personalities are all awaiting the painter's brush.

The figure used in this book was sculpted by Mike Stelzel and is produced by his company, Michael-Roberts Ltd. It is typical of the high quality of today's commercially produced military miniatures. I have a deep interest in the British colonial period and selected this figure for that reason. The figure is composed mainly of resin parts. While resin seems to be the trend, many companies use the traditional white metal alloy for their figures. I have worked with both and find very little difference in the two, except for a lighter weight with the resin castings.

I hope this book will inspire you to become interested in the rewarding hobby of painting military miniatures.

Chinese Boxer

STARTING YOUR FIGURE

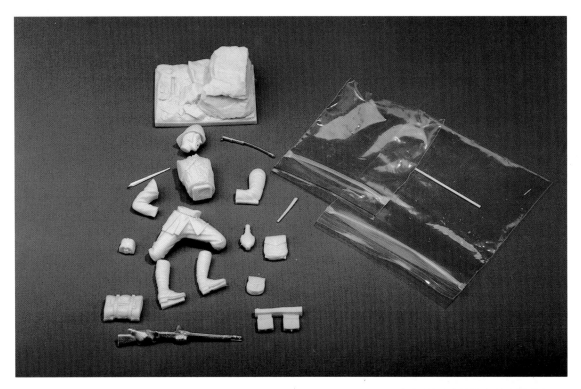

Commercially made kits for military miniatures typically come like this. They may have from one piece to twenty, made of either metal or resin.

The castings need to be cleaned up. One of the things you will need to work on are the seams that appear where two halves of the mold came together.

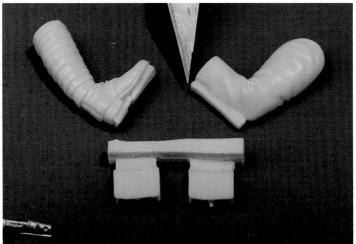

The other things that need to be removed are the carrier bars. These were used to carry resin into the mold and are seen here at the bottom of the boot and arm, and as a bar at the top of the belt bags. **BE CAREFUL!** Some things that look extra are really necessary for setting the figure on the base, or are part of the uniform. Do your research first.

The other thing you need to look for are places where the resin did not fill the mold leaving missing fingers or unwanted holes. If this happens take the model back to the store before you work on it. The higher the quality of the product the less often this will happen.

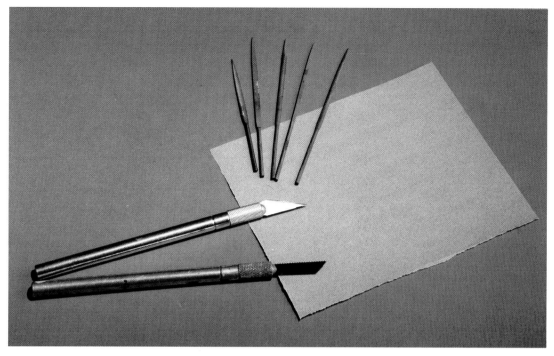

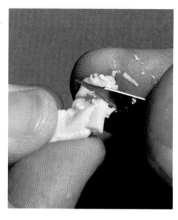

In the clean-up process, I do not use the knife for carving as much as for scraping. With the blade tilted toward me, I scrape it over the part I want to shape. It is a very effective method and gives much more control than carving.

The basic clean-up tools are a hobby knife, miniature razor saw blades for the knife, sandpaper, and a variety of small, hobby-sized files.

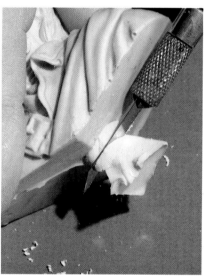

Big pieces like this can be sawed off.

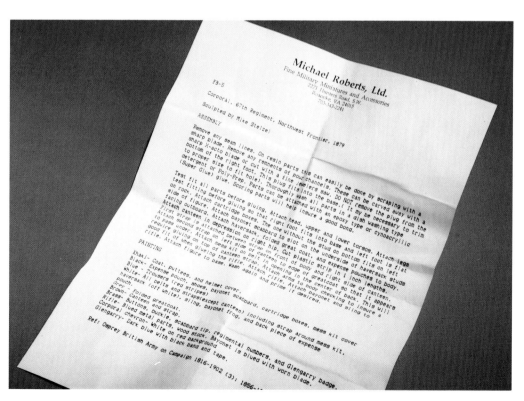

Before starting any work, review the painting and assembly instructions. They contain vital information.

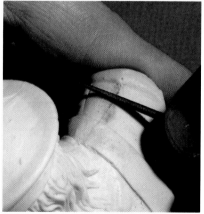

Light seam lines can be filed off. More severe lines may need to be scraped before filing.

Some larger areas, like the bottom of this display base, can be smoothed by running them with a circular motion over sandpaper.

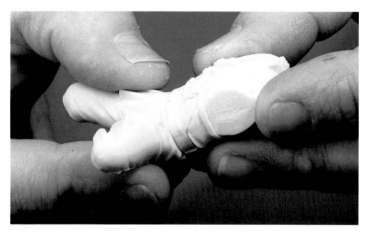

Test fit all the parts to make sure they parts join properly.

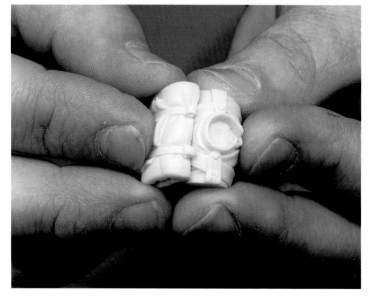

Hold the part in place...

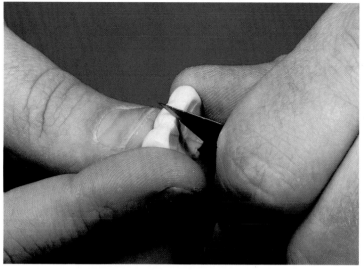

and make any necessary adjustments.

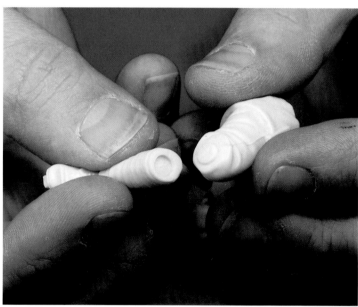

In the zeal for clean-up don't remove things that need to be here. An example is the bump at the knee of the figure. It could be mistaken for waste unless you take the time to see that it is really a connector rod for the lower leg.

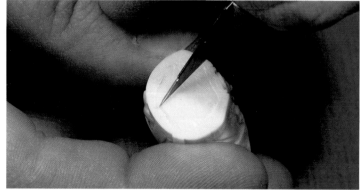

After the clean-up and fitting, you will want to create glue reservoirs in the major joints. This is done by creating a hollow in the center of the joint leaving a wall around, being sure you don't destroy any visible detail. I usually leave about 1/8" around the edge, if there is room.

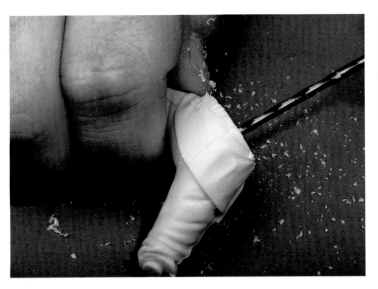

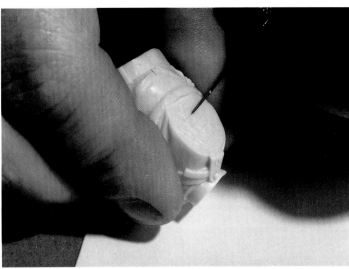

I also drill holes in these major joints to hold more glue. The number depends on the size of the surface. The depth doesn't need to be exact, but they are about 1/8" deep.

and upper body.

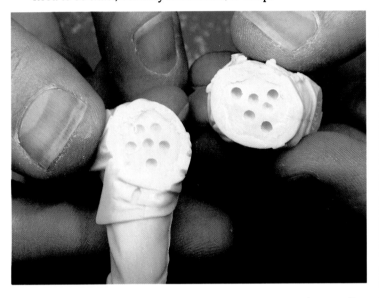

The waist joint can take this many holes. Smaller surfaces will take less.

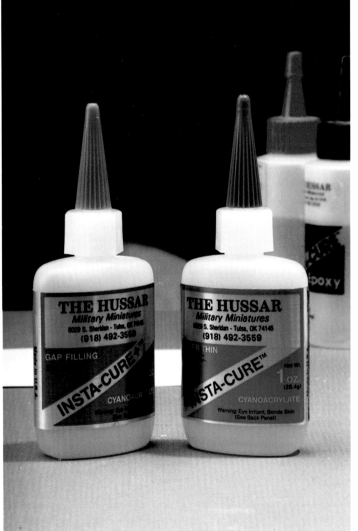

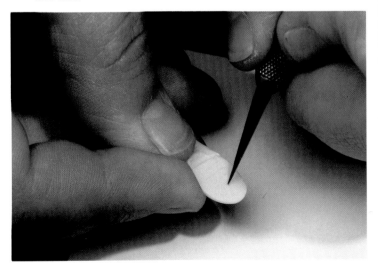

The bare minimum treatment of a glue joint is to cross hatch with the point of the knife. This is used on a shallow piece like this shoulder of the arm..

When the glue joints are prepared we move to gluing. Two types are available, cyanoacrylate (super glue)...

and mix thoroughly.

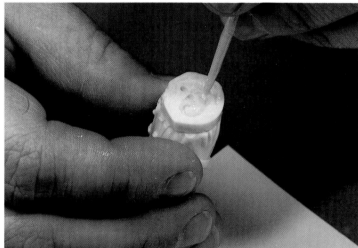

and epoxy. For resin the super glue seems to work as well as the epoxy. On metal, a five minute epoxy is what I recommend for the major portion of the figure. The super glue works well for the light weight items on metal figures.

I'm using 5 minute epoxy on the major joints. Work the glue into the holes of the joint surface.

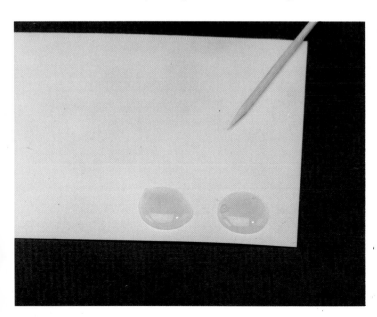

With the epoxy use equal amounts of the A & B parts...

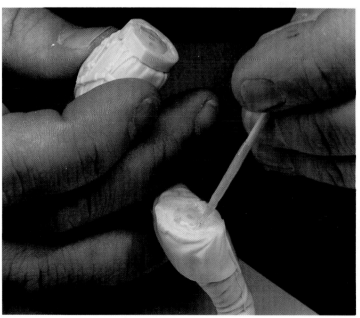

Apply glue to both surfaces. Keep the glue away from the edges.

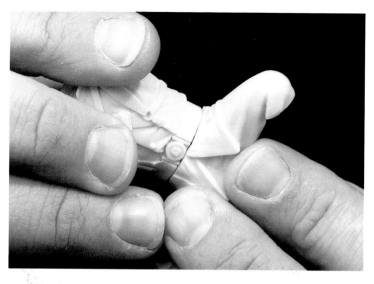

Check alignment front and back, left and right. Make sure the part is facing the correct way.

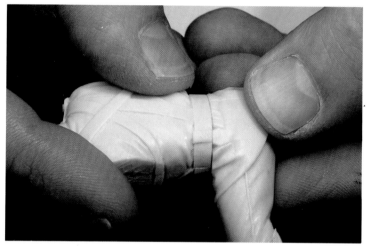

The alignment of straps is one good key. With the epoxy you need to hold the parts in place for five minutes. The maximum strength of the epoxy comes at about 30 minutes.

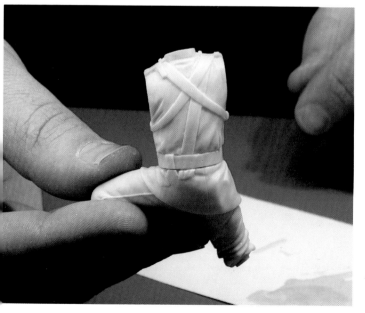

The gaps should be as minimal as possible, but there may need to be some filling with hobby filler putty.

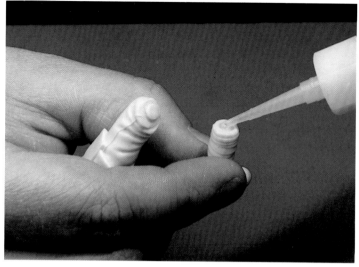

I use a slow drying super glue. This gives me a few seconds to make adjustments, which is important in spots where alignment is critical. The lower leg is such a spot. Apply the glue to one surface.

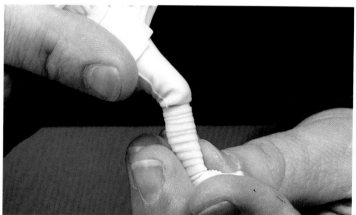

Join the lower leg to the upper and align. Observe the leg to make sure it appears to be in a natural position. Before you applied the glue you should have checked it with the base.

Follow the same gluing procedure with the second leg. Here I want to set it in place on the base while it is still pliable to make sure the position is correct. Look at it from every angle. Be sure the foot is carrying the pressure of the step in a natural way.

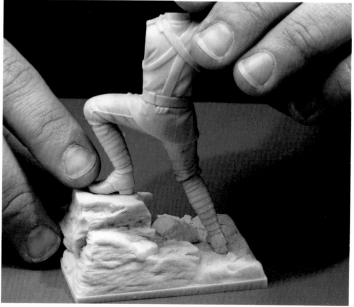

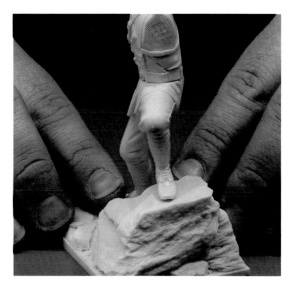

From the front you can see if the vertical alignment is correct.

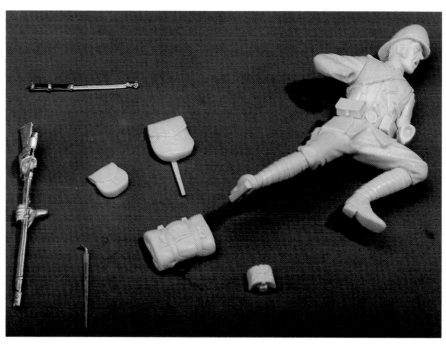

Go ahead and glue as much of the figure as is reasonable. You want to have good access for painting, so the body and some of the accessories will be painted before they are glued together.

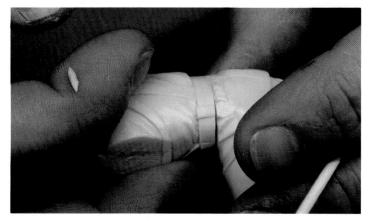

I use a two-part epoxy filler for the gaps. After blending it, I work it into a small snake...

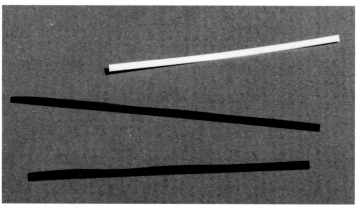

The kit comes with a piece of plastic to use for straps, but it is too stiff for my liking. I use electrical tape that has been dipped in paint thinner for a few moments to dissolve the adhesive, and has the glue wiped off. I cut it to the width of the piece provided in the kit.

The painter will have to decide whether to add the straps now or later. I have chosen to do it before painting. Use super glue to attach it to the body at the place where the molded strap ends. I do the hardest to reach spots first, like the canteen strap here in the front, under the figure's right arm. This continues the molded strap around the back.

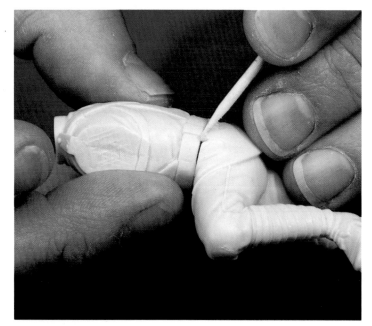

and force it into the gap so it follows the contours. When it sets, sand it into the proper shape.

10

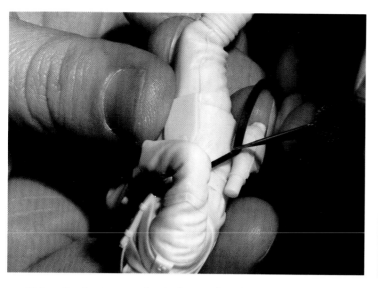
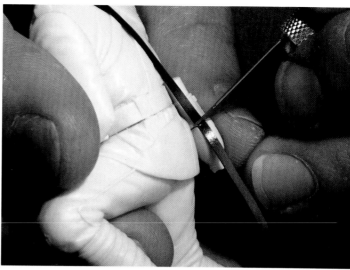

When the first connection is dry apply a dot to the next and use a knife to pull the tape taut. Hold it until it sets.

Use a knife to carefully slice off the excess.

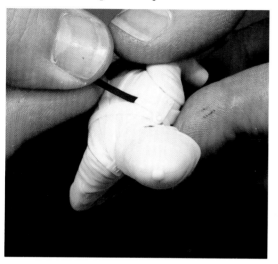
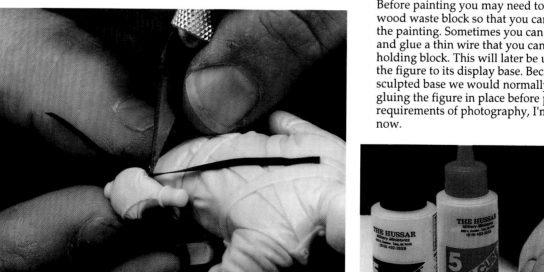

Repeat on the back, where the molded strap ends at the left shoulder.

I use a light gray or white spray on primer.

Before painting you may need to lightly tack the piece to a wood waste block so that you can hold it by the block during the painting. Sometimes you can drill into the leg of a figure and glue a thin wire that you can insert into the wood holding block. This will later be used to permanently connect the figure to its display base. Because this figure came with a sculpted base we would normally use that as a holding block, gluing the figure in place before painting. Because of the requirements of photography, I'm going to break this rule for now.

Again, push with the knife to create the tautness that signifies weight.

PAINTING YOUR FIGURE

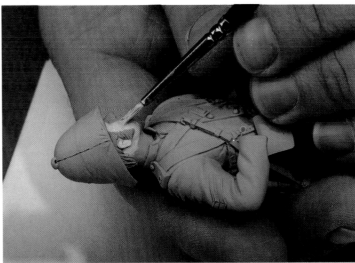

Lay the pieces on paper for priming. Hold the paint can about twelve inches from the object. Spray in short bursts going all the way across the object. Don't let the spray stay in one place for too long. Use a light hand when priming. Excessive amounts will obscure detail.

The undercoating is simply a smooth, thin coat with good coverage, using a color that is as near as possible to the color of the artist's oils that you will apply on top of it. I begin with flesh color for the hands and face.

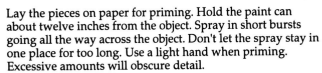

When the primer coat has thoroughly dried, we add an undercoat of color. For this step I use hobby paint for its covering ability. Usually I begin with the face and work my way out layer by layer. Either a water or oil based paint may be used if it is of good quality. I use a variety of brushes for painting, but for the undercoating I stick to either a 00 or 000 red sable brush.

You can continue with other colors as long as it isn't in a critical area, like a white strap going across a red jacket. Check your reference material for colors of uniforms, and find one that comes nearest. This fellow's uniform is khaki, but since khaki comes in many gradations, it is important to know exactly the color I want.

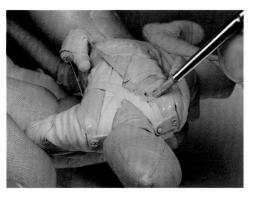

While it is not a problem if you overpaint the belts at this points, be careful to avoid paint build-up on small details.

The paints I use for the finishing paint are artist's oils. The face is the most important part of the figure. The colors and shading of the face use a pallet of white, burnt sienna or mars brown, yellow ochre, cadmium yellow, and cadmium red (in miniscule amounts).

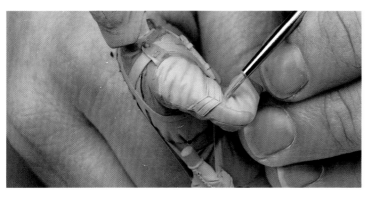

I know from the directions that the corporal stripes will be white with a red outline, so it is easier to cut around it than to try to cover it later.

Continue the undercoating until everything that needs it is complete.

I use three different shades of color for the figure. Every part will be covered with a middle tone of color, be it khaki, blue, or flesh. These colors will be darkened for shadows, and lightened to create highlights. The middle flesh tone is a mixture of white, yellow ochre, mars brown, and a small amount of cadmium yellow.

This is not an exact science, so each batch will be slightly different. I try to mix enough to do the whole figure. On the left is the flesh tone. On the right is straight mars brown which I will use for the darkest shadows.

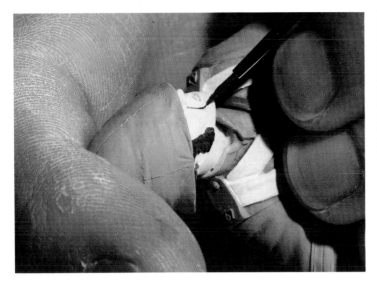

When the undercoat is completely dry, lay the mars brown into the deepest shadow lines. Thin the paints so they flow easily, but are not too runny. The shadow lines include the smile lines...

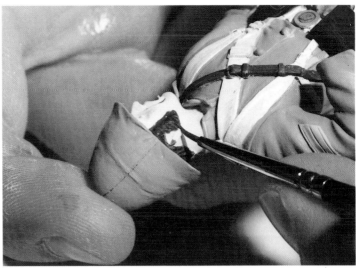

Go around any place where the skin meets hair...

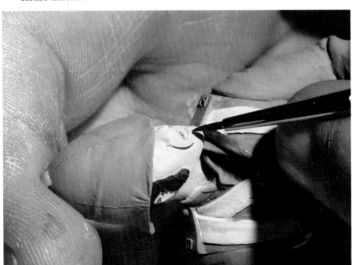

under the lower lip...

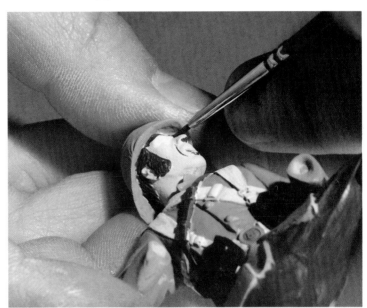

hat or any other area border of skin and something artificial.

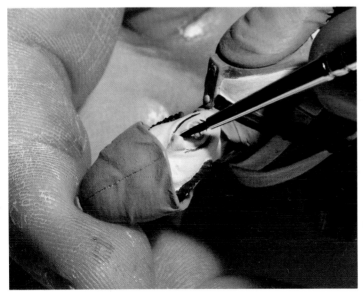

and under the nose.

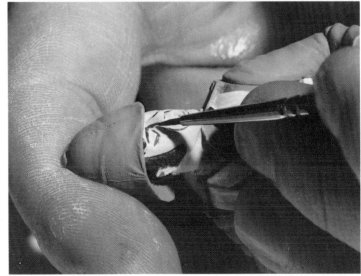

Paint along the side of the nose to the tear line and up over the eyelid. Also paint the bag of the eye underneath.

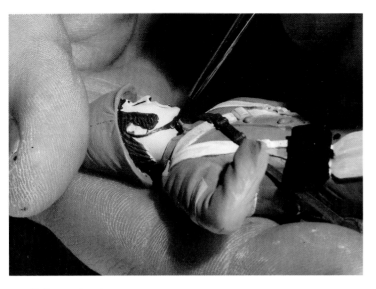

Paint under the jaw line.

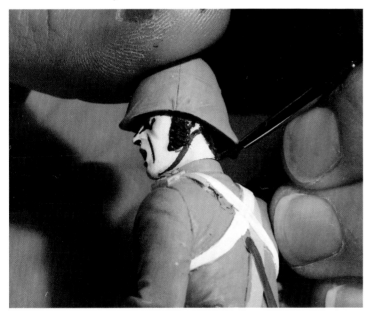

Paint the inside of the ear and around the collar.

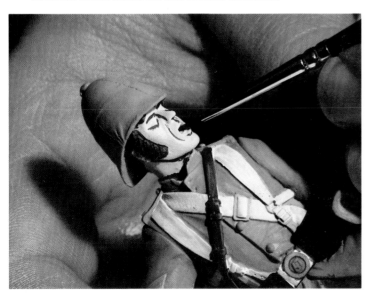

Because the mouth of this figure is open we can darken the inside.

Because of the drama of the mouth, we need another shadow outside of the smile line, denoting the ridge. These lines look very hard now, but do not worry. They will be blended as the painting continues.

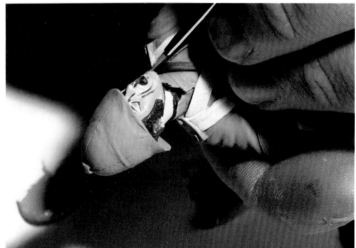

With the middle shade of flesh, paint up to the dark shadow lines. Don't blend yet. It is easier to get things looking right if everything is to a common point before blending begins.

To begin blending shadows and skin, clean your brush and pick up a little middle flesh color. With short strokes work the brush through the shadows. You don't want to spread the dark shadow color, but blend the flesh into it and soften the demarcation line.

15

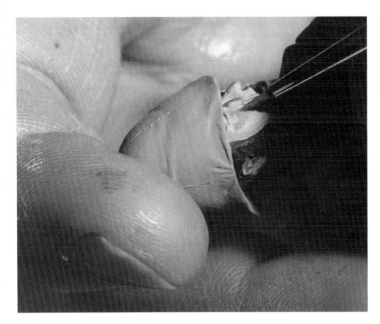

You want to be careful not to overwork the blending process, or you will lose the effect you are after. This is particularly true where two shadows are near each other, as in the parallel smile lines. These could easily become an indistinct blob rather than the folds caused by a grimace. If you do too much blending the oil paints are very forgiving, and you can go back in and reestablish the shadows. In fact, as a last step, after the middle tones and highlights, I go back and redo shadows as needed.

The blending has gotten rid of the hard lines, and left nice shadowed contours.

To get the highlight color I add white and just a touch of cadmium yellow. White tends to give the mixture a pasty effect, and the cadmium yellow brings it back to life. The highlight should be about 5 or 6 shades lighter than the middle color.

I usually test my color on the lightest part of the face, like the tip of the nose. I can fix it if it isn't just right.

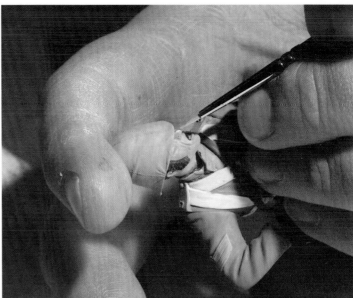

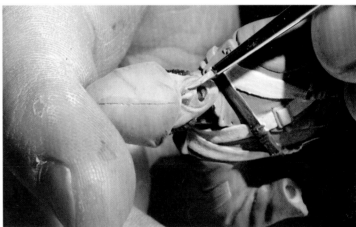

Highlight any raised areas that would reflect sunlight: the nostrils...

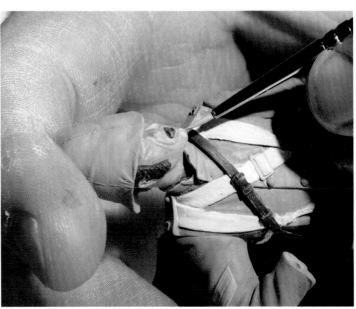

the chin...

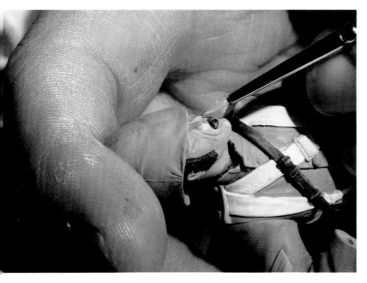

the outsides of the upper lip...

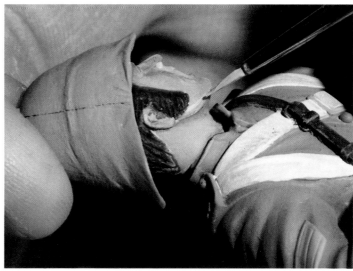

the jaw line...

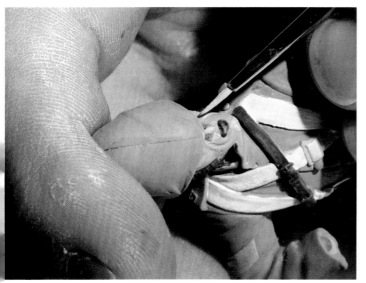

the ridge of the smile line...

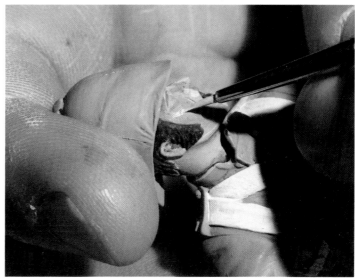

the cheek bone, in a crescent shape...

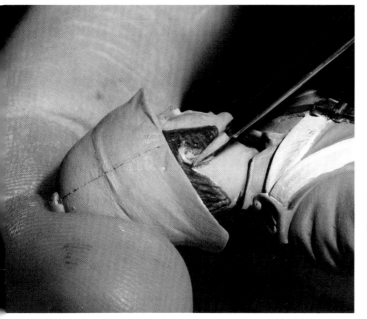

the tops of the ears, if exposed...

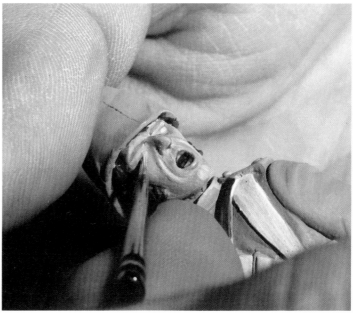

and the bag under the eye.

The result.

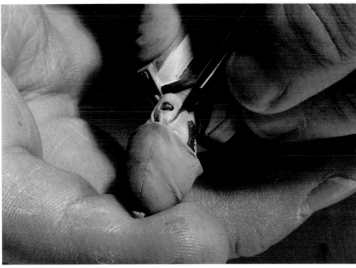

With a reshaped brush, go back over some of the shadow areas with a dark pigment. Use a light hand, as all you're trying to do is reemphasize it a little. This is only necessary in places where you may have overblended or eradicated the shadow.

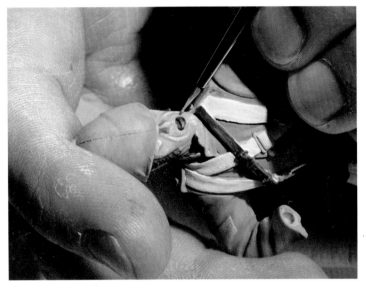

Selectively blend the highlights so you keep the shadows and skin tones. When I blend I think about the shape of the body part. When the mouth is open like this, for example, the center of the upper lip is the most prominent, so I blend from there down, leaving that the lightest. Don't pull it too far into the shadow or too far down the mouth. If you go too far you just make a ring of lighter flesh, instead of a highlight.

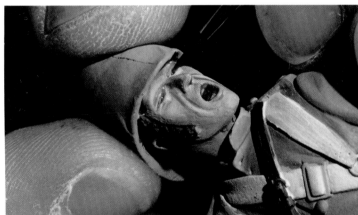

Use the dark pigment to cut in a slit for the eyes.

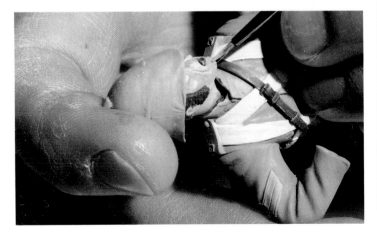

Continue blending. Remember to have a little of the blending color on the brush.

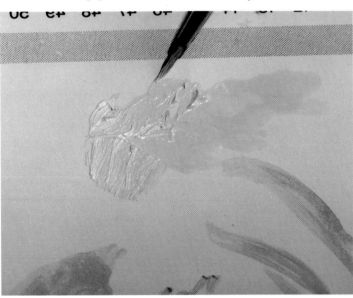

After the slit has dried somewhat we can paint the whites of the eyes. Just the tiniest tint of color should be added to the white to make it off white.

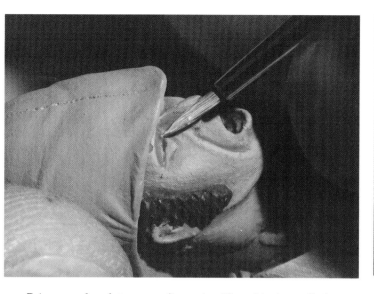

Bring your brush to a very fine point. The white is applied with a dot on the inside of the eye...

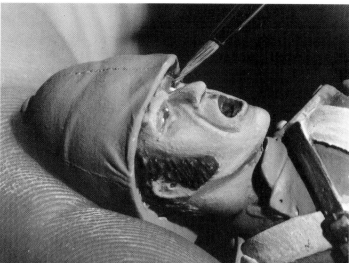

Simply go back to the medium flesh color and narrow the eye down.

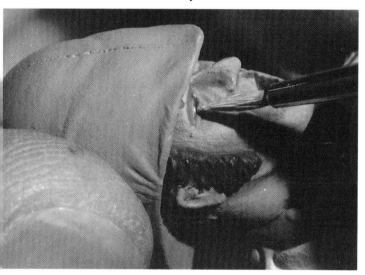

and a smaller dot on the outside.

The result.

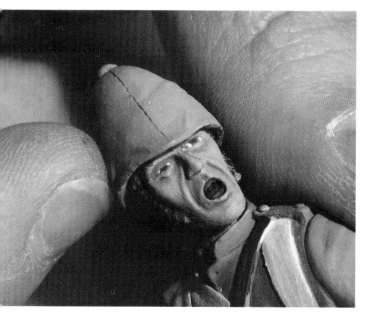

The result. Notice that the figure's left eye has a little too much white. This is a common problem and easily fixed.

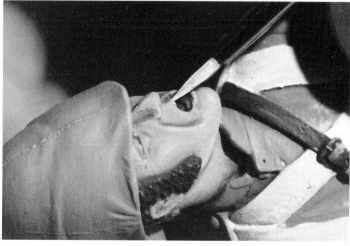

Use the same off white color for the teeth. While you don't try to create individual teeth, by using dots over the already dark base, you do create some sense of their separation. Do two or three dots at the top and at the bottom. In this model there is more room at the bottom, so we may use four or five teeth.

The result.

The hair can be done in a way similar to the face. I start with a dark color, then add a middle tone. Finally I add a highlight color. This is one of the few times where the undercoat acts as a deep shadow color because it will stay in the nooks and crannies. The middle tone is a mixture of mars brown and cadmium yellow.

A little cadmium red added to the flesh and shadow colors creates enough difference to make the tongue stand out.

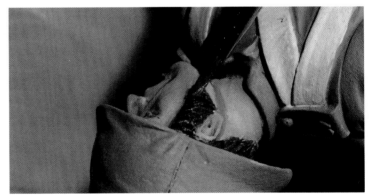

The hair is highly sculpted so I use a dry brush technique with the oils, going across the grain and catching the tops of the ridges with the middle tone brown.

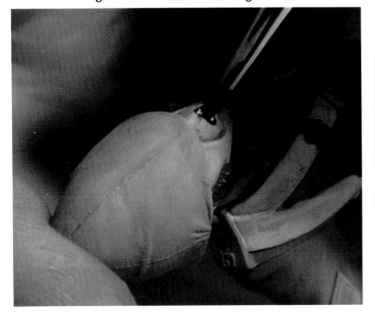

A dot on the tongue is all you need. It's almost like highlighting a shadow.

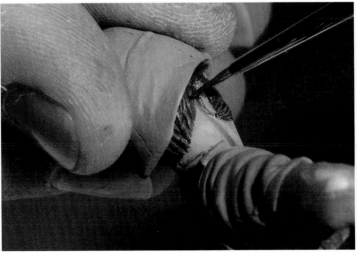

On the back of the head you can see how it is really picking up the color.

The highlight color is a mixture of the middle tone plus cadmium yellow and white.

Progress.

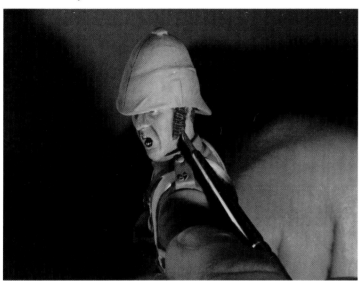

Apply the highlight color in the same way as the middle tones, but more lightly. If you stay to the middle of the sideburn or other contour, it gives more of a feeling of height.

The British khaki color of the helmet and uniform is mixed from burnt umber, sap green, yellow ochre, and white. There is a range of correct colors for khaki, so use your eyes. Don't use too much sap green or you will have olive instead of khaki. Mix the colors thoroughly. This is the middle tone.

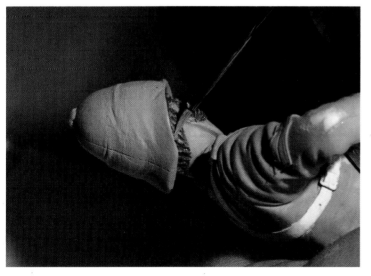

On the back use short, choppy strokes, again, going down the middle.

To this I add burnt umber to create my shadow tone.

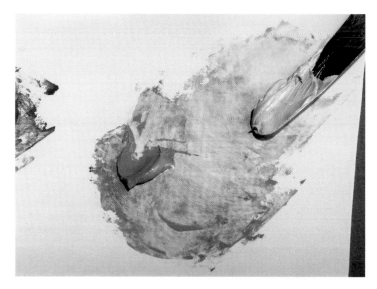

Add white to the medium tone to get the highlight tone.

Carefully paint the underside where the brim meets the head.

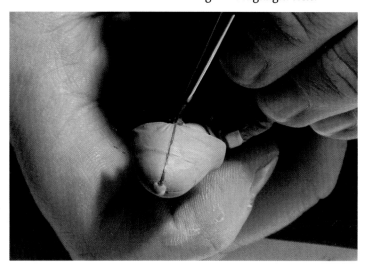

I begin by cutting in the shadow areas of the uniform. At the helmet we find four holes in the ventilator knob. Leading down from the knob are four seams where the four piece khaki covering of the pith helmet was sewn together. Paint the seams in the shadow tone.

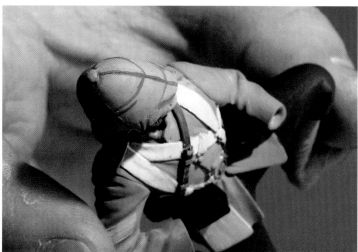

The helmet is ready for the middle tones.

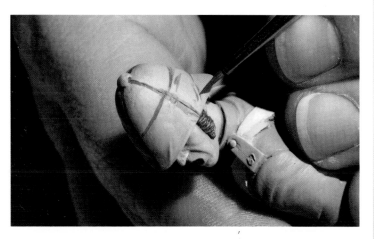

There is a pugree around the rim of the pith helmet under the covering. The wrinkles show through and should be shadowed. You will also find stress lines of the stretched fabric that should be shadowed. Fortunately the sculptor has put most of these lines in, so you don't have to create them as you go.

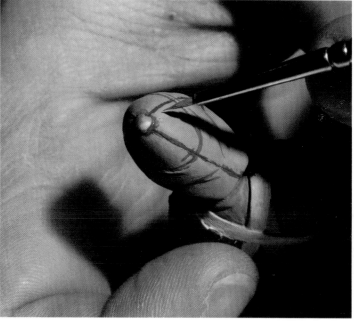

Add the middle tones working up to the shadow lines, but not over them for now.

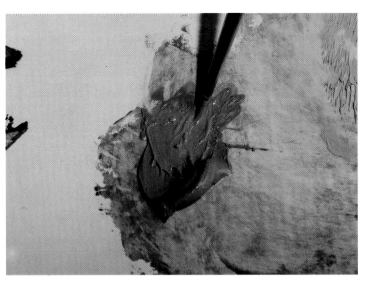

The middle tones applied.

The consistency of the paint may vary from brand to brand. To make it work you may have to make an adjustment with every new brushful. You want the paint to flow nicely off the brush. I like a consistency that covers well, but isn't running. If you have to drag your brush two or three times over the piece to get paint on it, the paint is probably too thick.

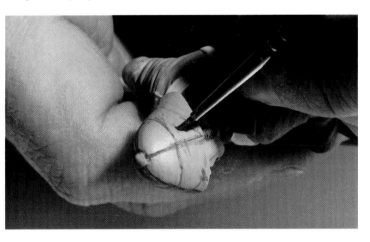

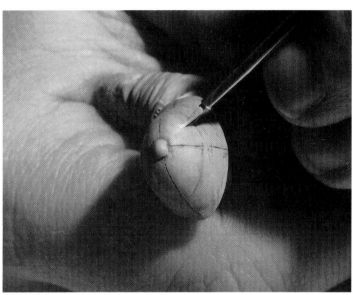

With a little medium pigment on your brush, blend the surface and the shadows.

Begin applying highlight to the highest points of the helmet.

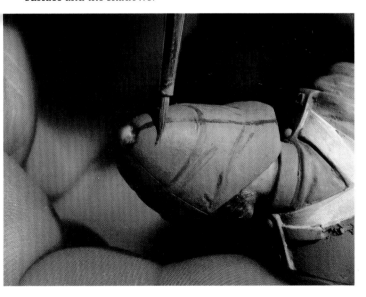

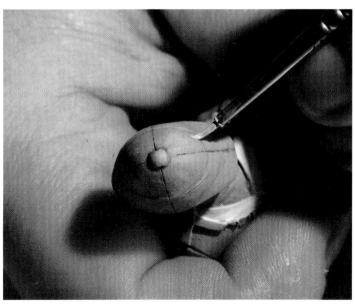

The seams between the sections of the helmet cover need to be reduced to a hint by using the middle tones.

Blend the highlights, following the contour of the helmet.

23

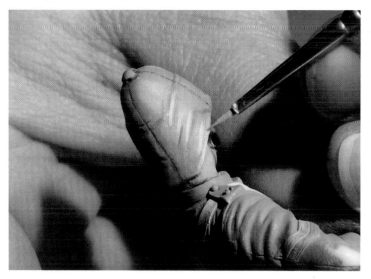

Highlight and blend the folds and the edge of the helmet.

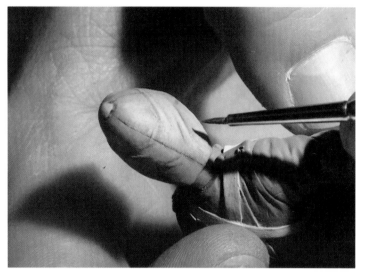

After highlighting go back and restore any shadows you may have obliterated and strengthen any that may need accentuation.

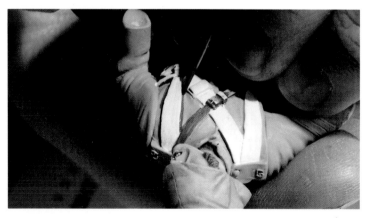

The process is almost the same on the jacket using the same colors. The purist might want to change the color of the khaki just slightly because, in reality, the hat cover and the jacket may have come from two different towns or dye vats and may have a slightly different shade. Also, I create a darker shadow color by adding burnt umber, to be used only where the belts meet the jackets. This gives a little lift and dimensionality to the belts. Apply this shadow first.

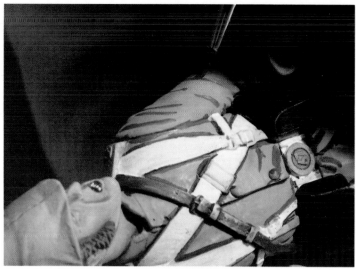

Hit the other folds, wrinkles, seams, the openings, under the epaulets, and around the corporal stripes with the regular shadow color.

I left the hands and feet off the model, so I could easily get to the chest and lower arms.

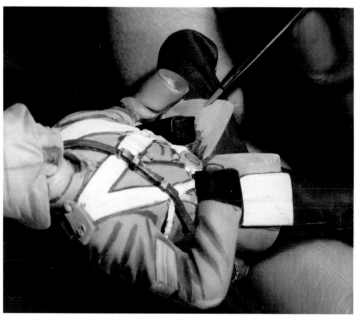

Go up to the shadow tones with the middle tone khaki.

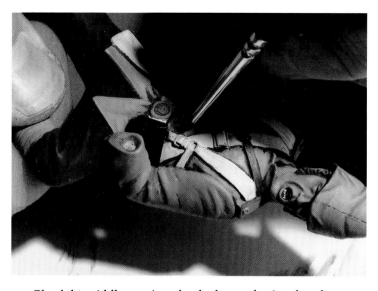

Blend the middle tone into the shadow, softening the edges.

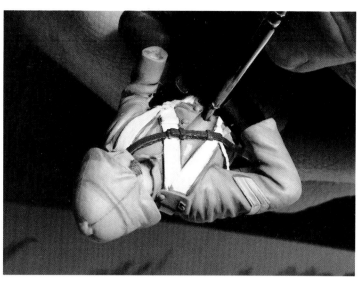

Blend the highlights. This softens the colors and helps add height and depth to the figure.

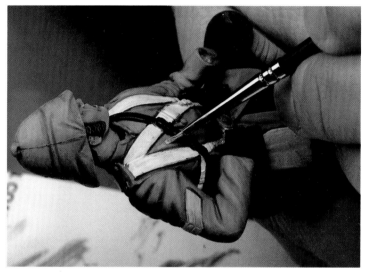

When adding highlighting I treat each area defined by the straps as a separate work area.

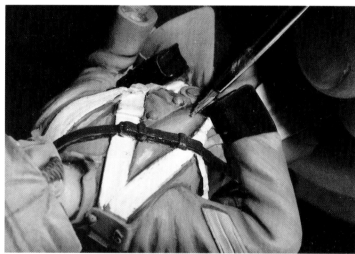

After blending I can go back with the highlight tone in a smaller area, to reinforce the look I'm after. You can keep doing this until you get it right; that is, until it looks right to you.

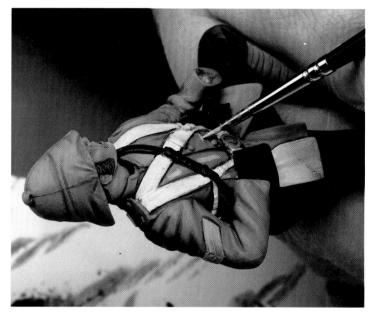

In this larger area I run a highlight down the center of one side, and on the top edge of the folds.

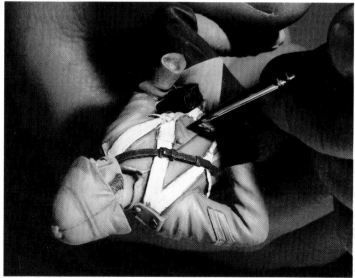

Stengthen any shadows that may have been taken away in further painting.

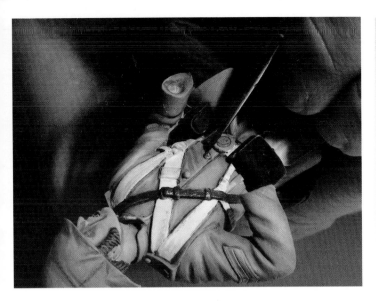

Undercoat the buckle and buttons with brown, which I use behind any gold metallic color. (I put black behind silver.) This helps create a shadow under the metal.

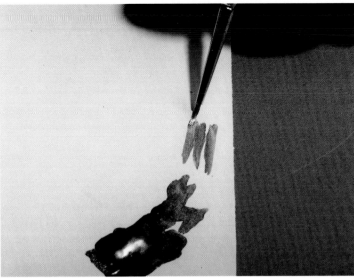

The regiment number, 67, is molded into the belt buckle, and to pick it up I use a dry brush technique. Load the brush with gold, then pull it out on paper until it is almost empty.

I never shake my metallic paints, as this creates swirls of thinner that are not desirable. Instead I pull pure pigment from the bottom of the can with a toothpick, and use the liquid at the top to thin it as necessary.

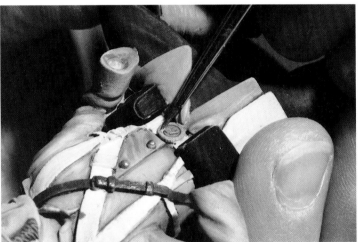

With the brush at a low angle go lightly over the buckle so only the high points pick up the paint.

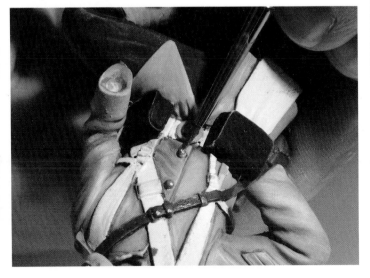

For the buttons thin the paint to a flowable state and touch the brush to the button to leave a dot of gold.

The result. The brown undercoating helps bring out the gold.

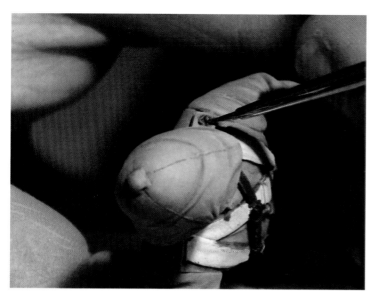

Repeat the process on the regiment numbers on the epaulets. I'm doing these now because I have the paint out. If they get overpainted later, I just do them again.

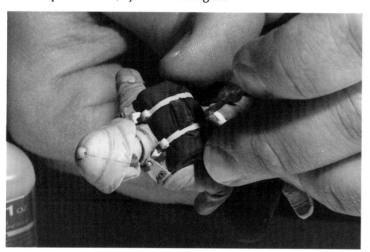

Attach the accessories at the appropriate places, as specified in the instructions. These have all been undercoated before assembly. Test fit before gluing them in place. These could have been glued on at any time, but they weren't because painting straps and other details were easier without them.

Before attaching the rifle and hands I will paint the back side, which will be difficult to reach later. Use burnt sienna or mars brown with red and yellow added to it to give it an orange tint. The color is an artist's choice since colors varied from dark to almost a bright orange.

Apply to the gun stock.

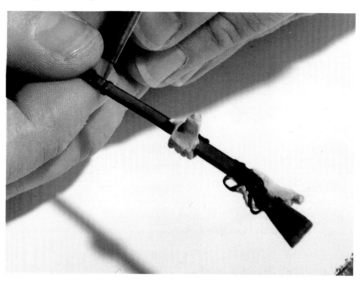

This end piece can wait until after assembly since it will be accessible. Of course, if you want, you could paint the whole rifle before you paint anything else. It's up to you.

For highlighting you simply add white and perhaps a little bit of red and yellow if you want to orange it up.

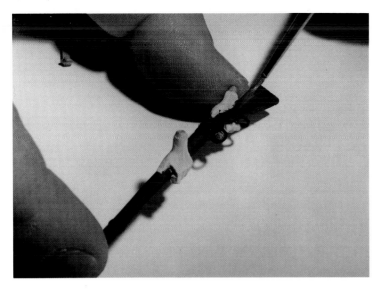

Hit the high points with the highlight.

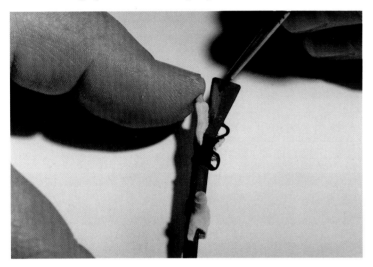

Soften the edges, always working toward the highlight.

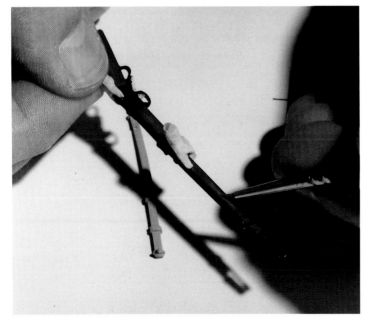

In the narrow parts I stay in the center and lightly highlight. These little things may not seem like much, but they make a great difference in the overall appearance of realism.

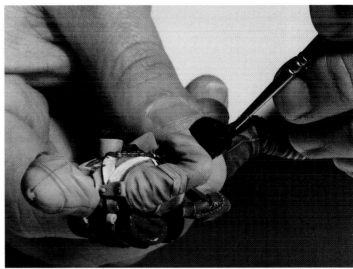

We need to paint the accessories before we attach the gun. They are black leather and are undercoated in black. Over this we paint everything with black oil. As the blending process continues this will become the shadow color in the folds and creases.

Because they are leather I mix mars brown with the black as a highlight color.

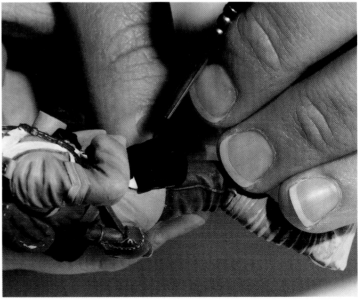

Apply the highlight to the centers of the large areas and the edges of the fold. This is a pretty liberal application because we want to leave pure black only in the deep shadows.

On the pouches add highlight to the edges where they would get a lot of wear, and to the middle of the top and other large areas.

This is applied more selectively, hitting only the spots that would experience the most wear, like the top and the edges of the flaps.

Blend the highlights. This is a very subtle shading. The trick is to change the black to give it life, but still keep it black in the mind's eye.

Repaint the undercoat of white on the straps to cover any stray paint from subsequent painting processes. Colors bleed through white easily, so this will help seal the mistakes.

The lightest highlight is made by adding more brown, taking it 4 or 5 shades lighter.

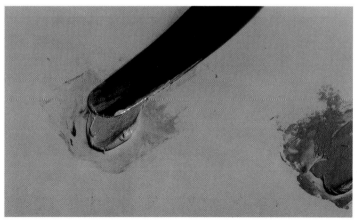

White has color variables with subtle differences. The highlights are the purest white, with other shadings being slightly offwhite by degrees.

I'm going to darken white with a miniscule amount of burnt umber. As you can see I also tried a little of my midtone uniform color mixed with the white. In truth you can blend what is pleasing to your eye, and my color schemes sometimes vary from figure to figure. This is the middle color.

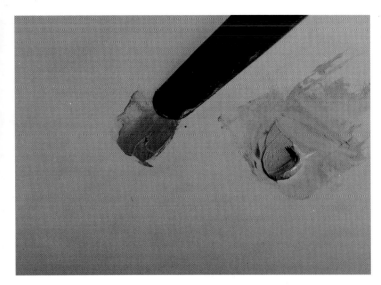

A little more burnt umber creates a color we use for outlining where one strap crosses another.

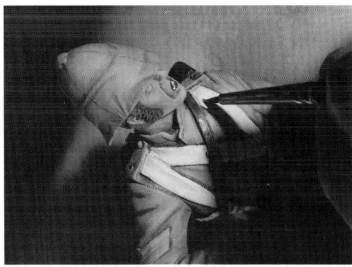

Soften the edges, blending slightly with the darker shade.

Begin with the darker color and just apply it at the edge where one strap goes under another.

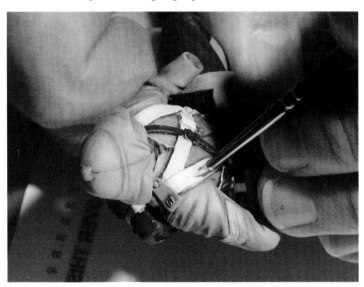

Pure white adds at the highlight. There is a lot of light at the shoulder. I like to highlight at the edges of belts and straps, leaving the middle less so.

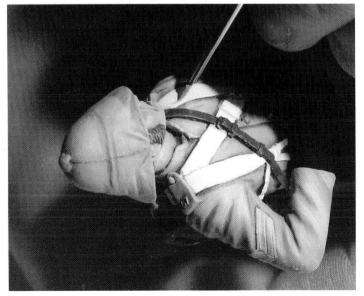

Apply the middle tone over the whole belt, going up to the darker color but not through it.

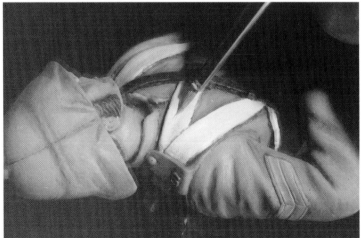

The strap of the haversack is listed as being off white, as opposed to the white of the suspension straps. You can either mix another color, or use less highlighting, as I have chosen to do. This slight difference will add a lot of interest to the figure.

Here you can see the contrast in the straps.

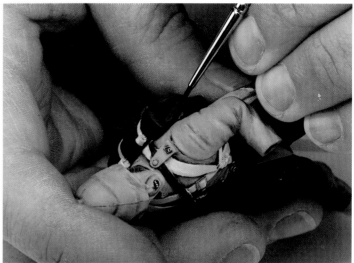

Lay the shadow tone in the folds and wrinkles.

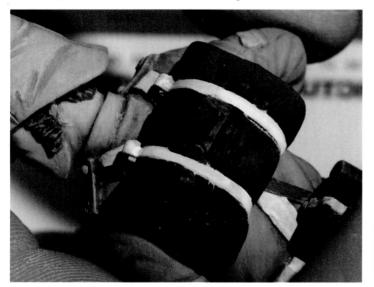

On the back is the grey great coat rolled up, with a glengarry exposed at the back of the resulting pack. The undercoat of the great coat is dark grey with white straps. The glengarry is dark blue hobby paint with a band of the glengarry and the tape that hangs off the back painted in black.

Outline the glengarry and the straps with same shadow tone, framing and boxing them in.

The color of the great coat will be a dark gray with a blue tint to it. I'm going to use a blue black tube paint, but if I didn't have that I would mix black and dark blue. This will be the shadow color, with white added for the middle color, and more white for the highlight color.

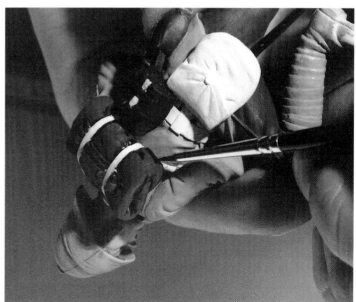

Hit the area where it turns back under at the bottom.

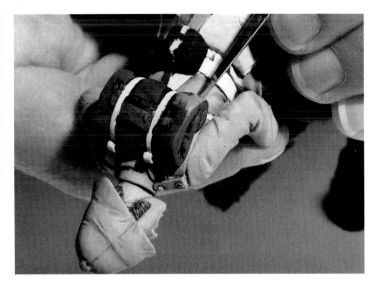

Add the middle tone to the great coat painting up to the shadow lines.

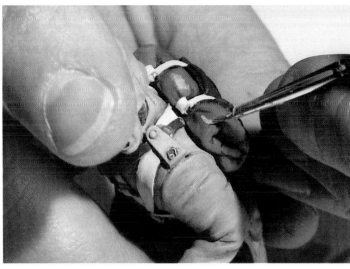

Apply the highlights.

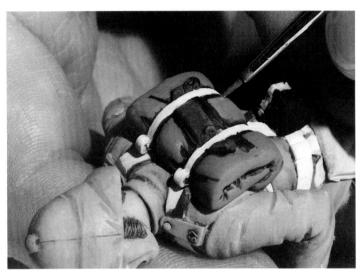

Soften the edges and blend the middle tone and the shadows, keeping a little of the middle tint in your brush.

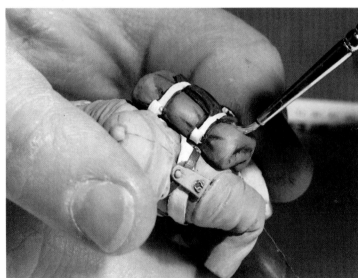

Blend the highlights.

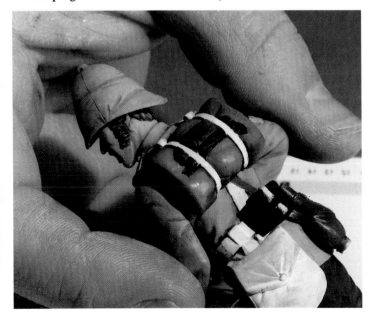

Progress.

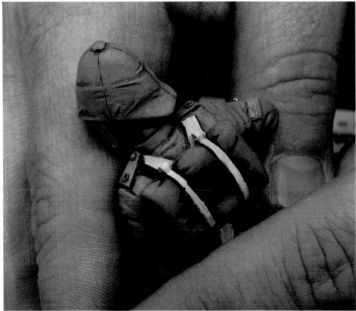

The highlights blended in.

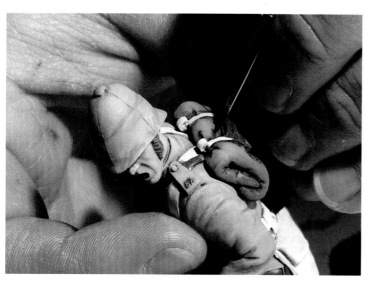

Go back and make refinements, darkening areas that got too light during the highlighting process.

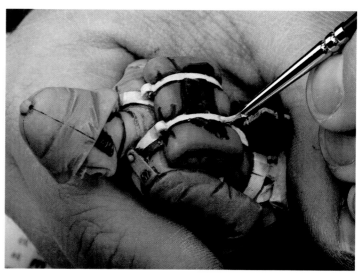

Apply offwhite to the main part of the belt and blend with the shadows.

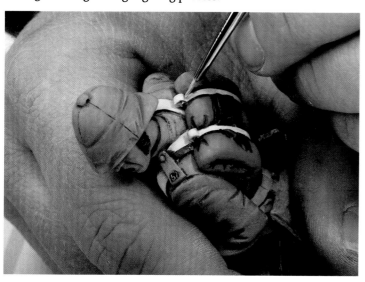

The white belts are painted just like the belts on the uniform, using a darker shade to define where belts cross...

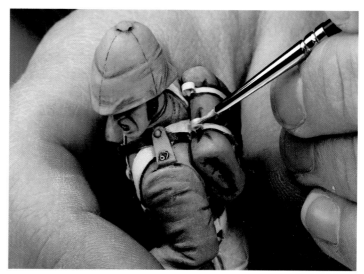

Add pure white to the tops of the rolled straps and any other place that would catch the light.

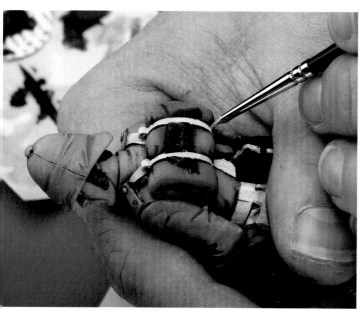

and on the underside.

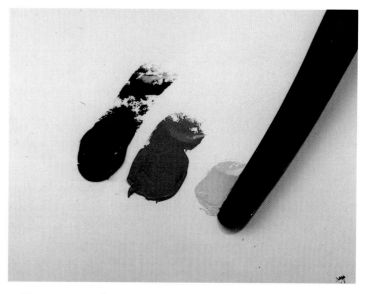

The canteen and canteen strap are undercoated in brown, to which we will add a mixture of mars brown, red and a small amount of yellow for the russet leather.

To this mixture I add mars brown for the darker shadow tone, and yellow with a touch of white for the highlights.

On the straps, paint the middle tones in the center sections, leaving the darker tones near the buckles and ends.

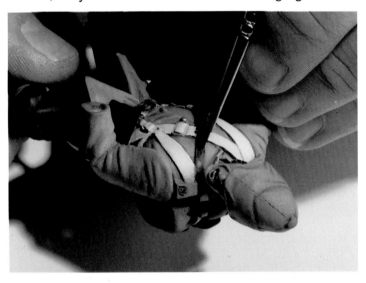

Apply the dark brown to the shadows...

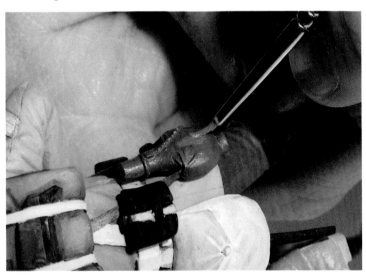

Highlight the edges of the folds, and apply the lighter tone to the center and work it out toward the edge.

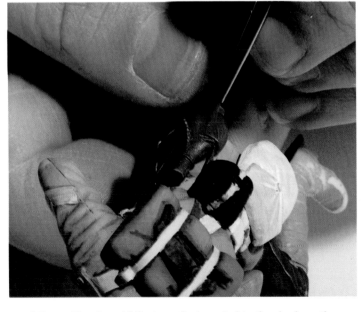

followed by the middle tone, first carried to the shadow, then blended in to soften the edges.

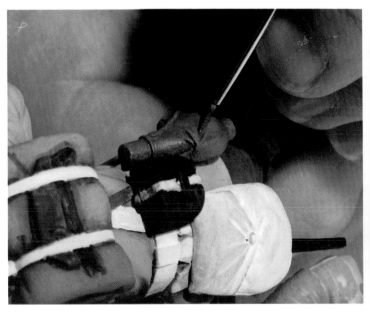

Go back and darken where necessary.

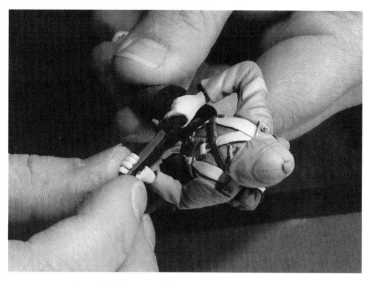

Glue the hand/rifle assembly in place. I would use epoxy for this joint, because of its stronger bond.

where the wrist meets the coat...

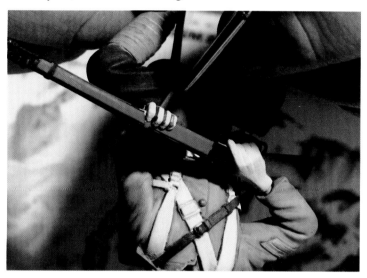

Paint the hands, using the dark flesh shadow between the fingers, and at the cuff, where the skin disappears beneath the clothing. The amount of shadow depends on the position of the hands, whether they are up or down, clenched or open. The flesh color you use on the hands does not need to be the same as that you used on the face. Often they are colored quite differently, so don't worry if you used up the first batch on the face. Just make some more that is a similar shade.

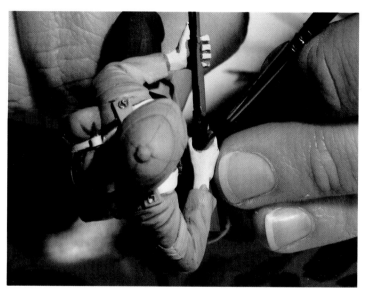

and where the hand meets the rifle.

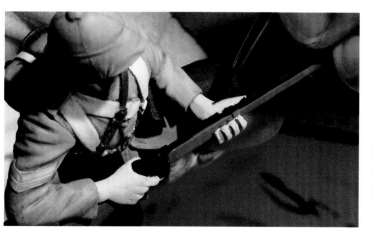

Darken where the thumb meets the wrist...

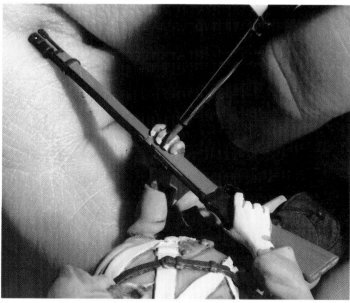

Paint everywhere else with the middle flesh color, coming up to the shadows.

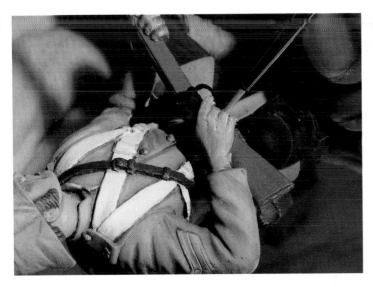

Blend the middle tones with the shadows.

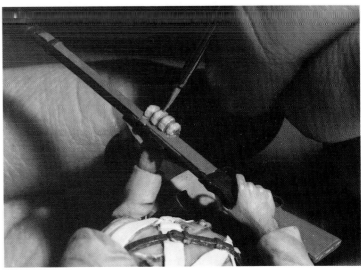

Blend the highlights in.

Highlight selectively, hitting the high points, like the top of the knuckles...

The back of this hand was molded flat, but you can see that, by pulling highlight and shadow into it, you give it dimensionality.

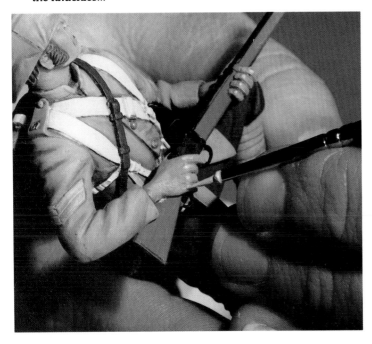

and the top of the fingers of the right hand.

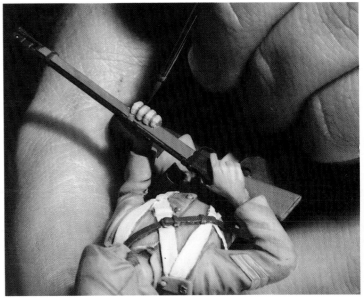

Go back and strengthen any shadows that may have been overblended.

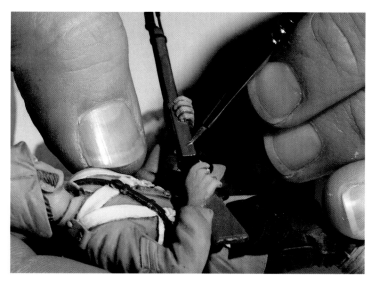

Paint the front side of the rifle as you did the back.

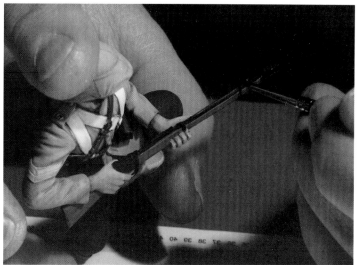

Use the same dry brush technique you used on the belt buckle to leave a highlight of silver on the high spots of the rifle. You can do this on the top of the barrel, the receiver group, and the cocking lever.

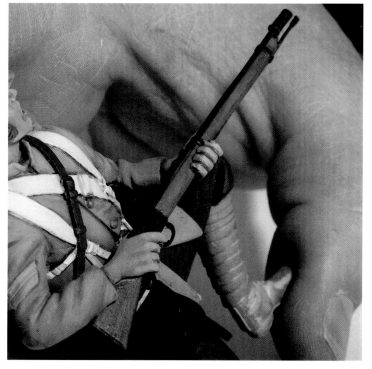

The rifle stock and hands completed.

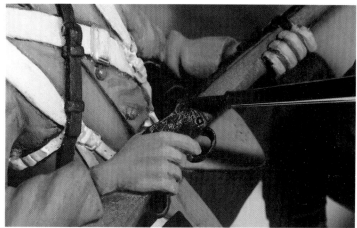

Sculpted screws will pick up the silver paint on the top. With the dark undercoat as shadow they come alive.

For undercoating of gunmetal you can use black or a premixed gunmetal color. For the overcoat I use artist's oil black, indigo, and a metallic silver, which can be a oil based hobby paint. The indigo is so dark that you can hardly see it when mixed with black. But when the silver is added you get a metallic blue black, which is perfect for this type weapon. (One other option with cast metal guns, is to simply add a black wash and burnish the metal to show through naturally.)

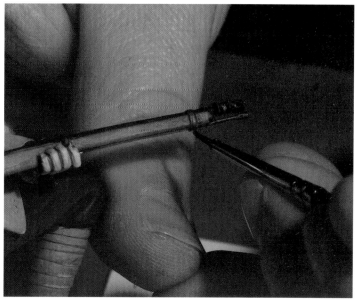

Paint the metal bands that hold the barrel to the stock.

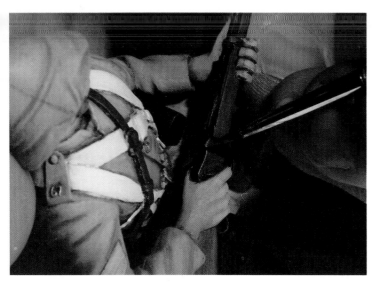

On the worn areas, like the top of the barrel and the edges of the receiver group, add highlight with pure hobby silver or steel color.

The pants are a very dark blue. For the shadow I use straight blue black or black. To this I add indigo and with a touch of white, to keep the middle tone a nice blue, though lighter than the shadow. To the middle tone I add a little more white for the highlights.

With the shadow tone cut in the folds and wrinkles and along each side of the welt.

Outline where the shadow meets the jacket and the puttees.

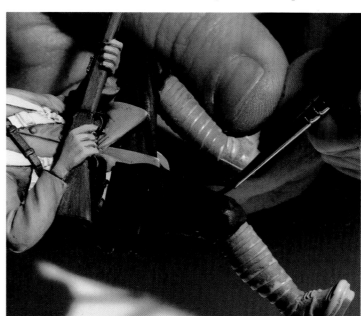

Cut in the middle color up to the dark colors...

then blend them, softening the edges.

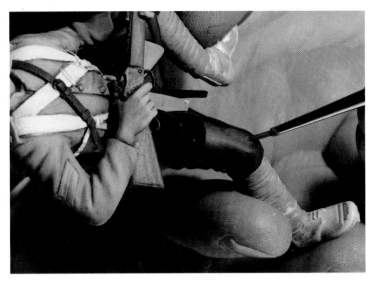

The first area to apply your highlight is the top of the leg. This will obviously pick up light, and if you need to adjust color, it is an easy place to do it.

On combat soldiers I often add some of the dirt of battle with the highlights. I add a little of the color of the base, in this case an arid brown, to the highlight color.

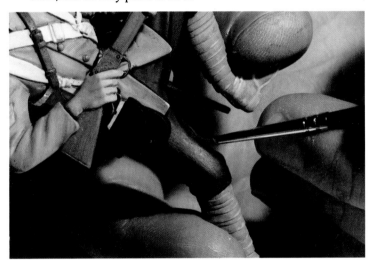

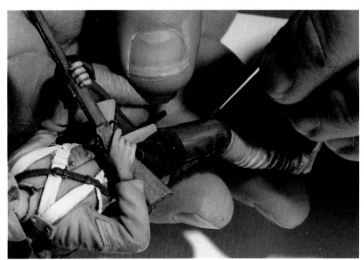

When the color is correct go back and highlight the folds and other prominent spots.

Apply it to the knee and other areas where he may have had contact with the soil. This is a selective and subtle highlight, and you may not even notice it until it is tied in with the base, but it does add realism.

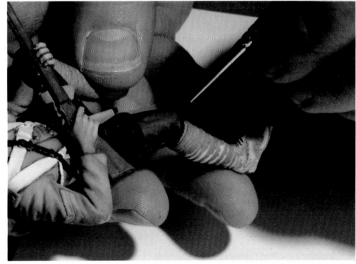

Blend the highlight tones.

Blend the dirty highlight, keeping it only to the logical areas that would come in contact with the dirt.

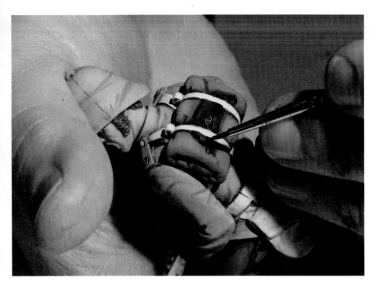

While you are using the colors for the pants, go to the back and do the glengarry. Cut in the straight black into the wrinkles and edges.

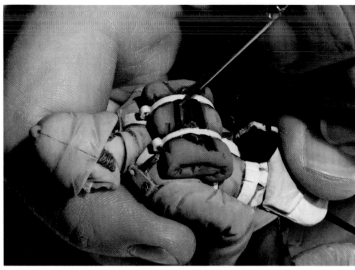

A slight highlight along the top edges is all it needs, followed by a blending.

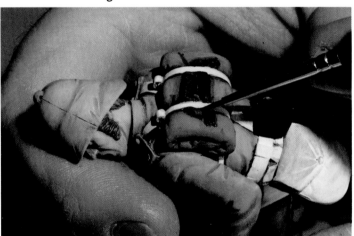

Continue with the black on the hat band and the tapes

Because the hat band and tape are cloth instead of leather, I add yellow ochre to the black to create the highlight rather than mars brown.

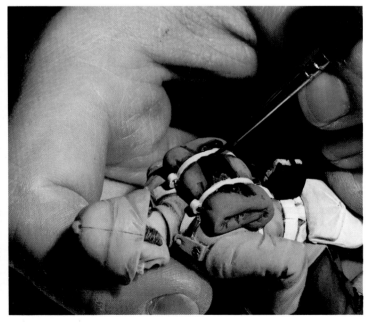

With the middle blue paint up to the black, then blend it with the shadows. The band and tape stay black.

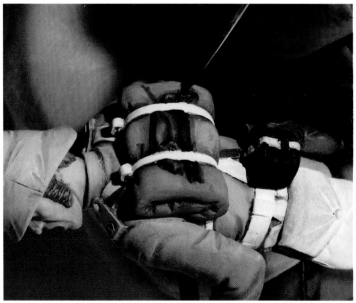

Use this to touch the highest points, leaving the rest alone.

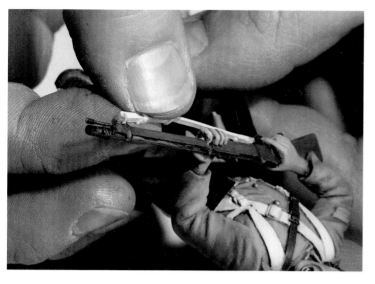

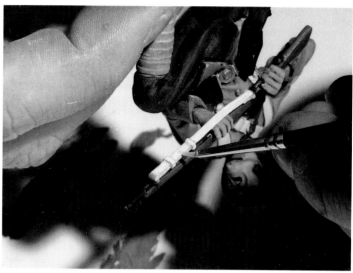

Glue the undercoated rifle sling to the gun. This will be white leather with metal swivels at each end.

Cut in the middle tone, then blend.

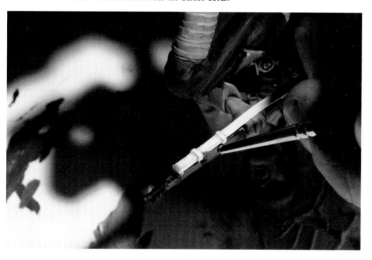

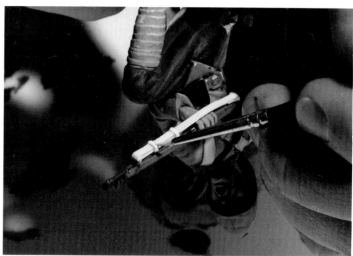

The rifle strap is painted in the same way as the suspension straps of the uniform. Put the darkest offwhite color along side any raised areas like these slip loops.

Pure white highlights the raised areas...

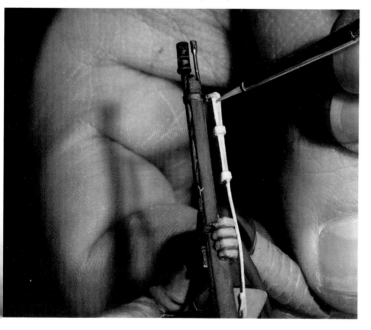

Where the strap doubles back, mark between the two layers.

and the middle area of each strap segment.

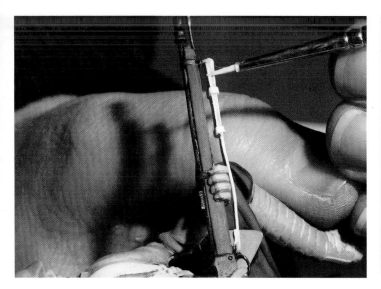

Use a dry brush stroke to lighten the leading edges.

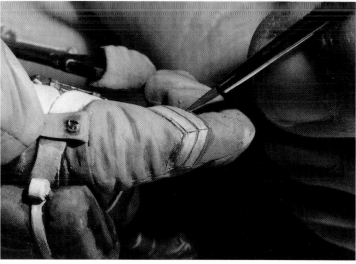

The raised outside perimeter has to be painted normally. The red will need to thoroughly dry before adding the white.

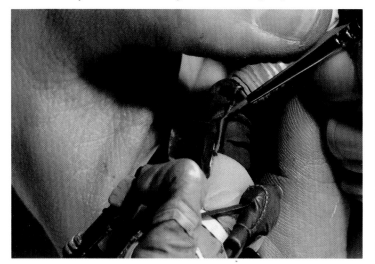

For real thin lines like the welt and the red of the corporal stripes, there is no way to highlight or shadow, so you may as well use straight hobby paint for micro-thin lines. They cover much better than oils, so you won't have to go over the area again and again. This is a nice bright red.

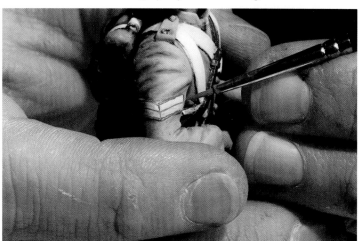

The result.

The corporal stripes are white with red outlines. The sculptor has put fine incised cuts on the outlines, so if you dilute your paint to a wash, and touch it to the junctures of the line, it will run the line. This will take a lot of control, which comes from a lot of practice.

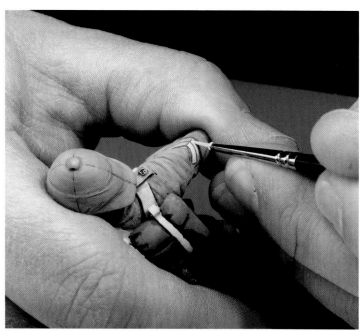

When the red outlines are dry, add a slightly off-white paint to the stripes.

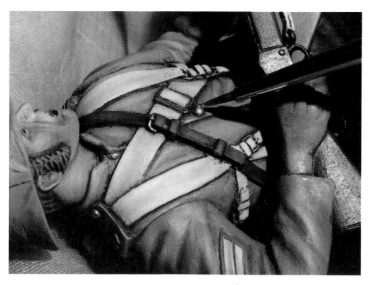

The buckles and buttons can be done at any time, in fact some painters prefer to save them for last. Again, use pigment from the bottom of the metallic paint container. Touch the buttons, the buckles...

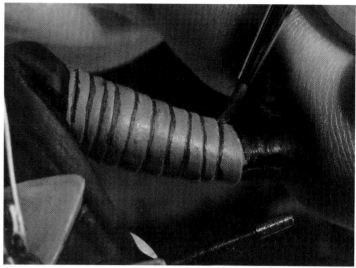

The puttees are painted in the basic khaki pallet, though it can vary slightly from the jacket. Apply the shadow shade to the edges of the wrappings, where one overlaps the next.

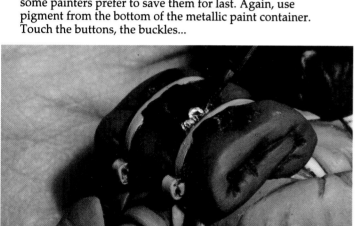

and the regimental cap badge on the glengarry.

Apply the middle khaki tone, working back to the shadows.

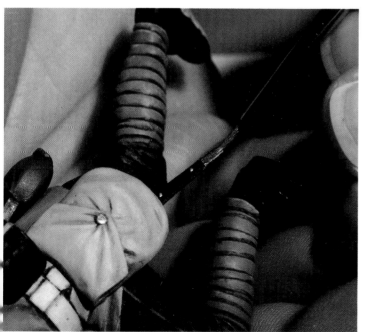

A touch of silver paint mixed with blue or blue black makes a steel color for the tip of the scabbard.

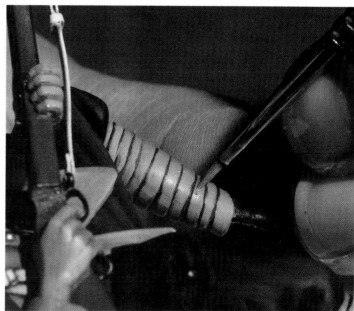

Blend to soften the demarcation line, but not too much. You want to keep a nice sharp shadow line on the puttees so each wrapping remains distinct.

Add some selective highlights. I just lay a line in the middle of each wrap and blend it in. I try to work down on this because the shadow comes at the bottom of each wrap.

Fix any areas that have been overblended.

The boots are painted like the black leather pouches. Over a black undercoat, we apply black oil paint. For the middle tones I add brown to the black, and even more brown for the highlight. The more brown you add to the highlight the more worn the shoe will appear.

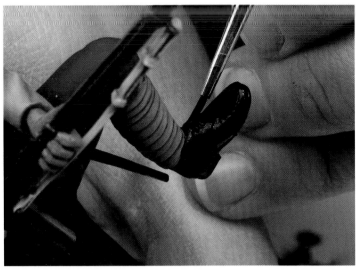

Apply the black oil to the whole surface.

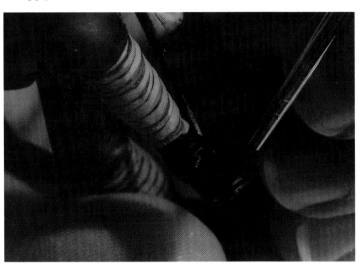

I start applying the middle color to the toes. Because these would normally be worn, I can test my color, and correct it if it is too light.

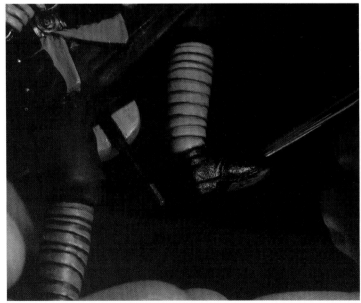

Apply the middle color all over the shoe, except in the folds where the straight black will become the shadow.

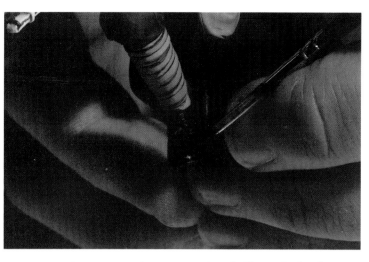

Because he is in an action pose, and probably on the battle field, I will do the highlight much more heavily than I would on a pair of dress shoes or than I did on the pouches.

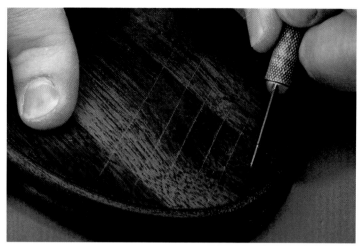

Because this base has a finish, I cross hatch it to assure adhesion of the groundwork.

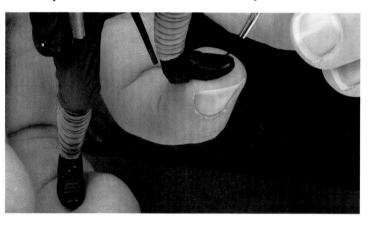

Feather and blend the highlight to show wear at the edges. Work it to follow the natural contour of the shoe.

I set the base back on the oval so the bayonet will not extend beyond the base, and add rocks in front of it to fill the void. Glue them in place with either epoxy or super glue.

Most painters will want to use the base to set the figure off and establish the mood of the piece. I've chosen to incorporate the base that came with the figure into a larger setting mounted on a wooden oval. You can be as creative as you like, but don't overpower the figure by having a base that is too large. The oval shape will protect the protruding and fragile bayonet. Since the provided base is smaller than the oval, I am going to add other groundwork to camouflage the rectangular base and tie the whole thing together. I use small rocks and Durhams Water Putty to build the environment.

You can mix the Water Putty as thick as you want. For the ground-work I want it fairly thick so it won't run off the base and will stay where I put it. Don't mix too much at a time, or it will set up before you can use it.

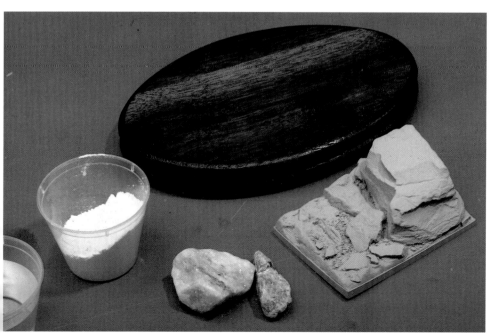

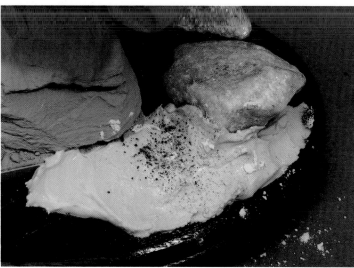

Start applying the putty around the glued elements of the groundwork. With a little water you can keep the putty workable until you get it blended into the other elements.

To simulate stones and pebbles I use dirt that has had all debris taken out of it or H-O railroad ballast. This will simulate small pebbles and stones. Sprinkle these on in certain areas.

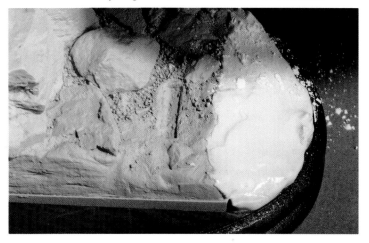

If the surface is too smooth from working it, you can sprinkle some dry putty on it in a random pattern. I work in small areas so I have plenty of time.

Make sure you camoflage the corners of the base that was provided with the kit.

Rocks should appear to emerge from the ground, so we work around them after they are glued. A dampened toothpick will help you get into the nooks and crannies.

A finished base with the groundwork melded in.

Decide the color you will want. This soldier is in Afghanistan, an arid area, so I want to paint the base in sand tones. Begin with the deepest color of the base, the shadow tone, as an undercoat. Any kind of hobby paint will work well, as will a larger sized brush. Undercoat the entire base.

By lightly dragging the brush across the surface you start picking up just the raised highlights. This highlighting goes over the whole base. Lighter highlights will go in smaller, more selective spots.

Add white paint to the undercoat paint to lighten it for highlighting. It needs to be quite a few shades lighter to create a good contrast. Load your brush...

With a lighter highlight, hit the hard edges and the upper-most surface of the base.

then wipe off the excess until there almost nothing coming off of it.

I basically leave the ground alone, but do add this lighter highlight to the rocks. You can add vegetation and other details if you wish.

THE GALLERY

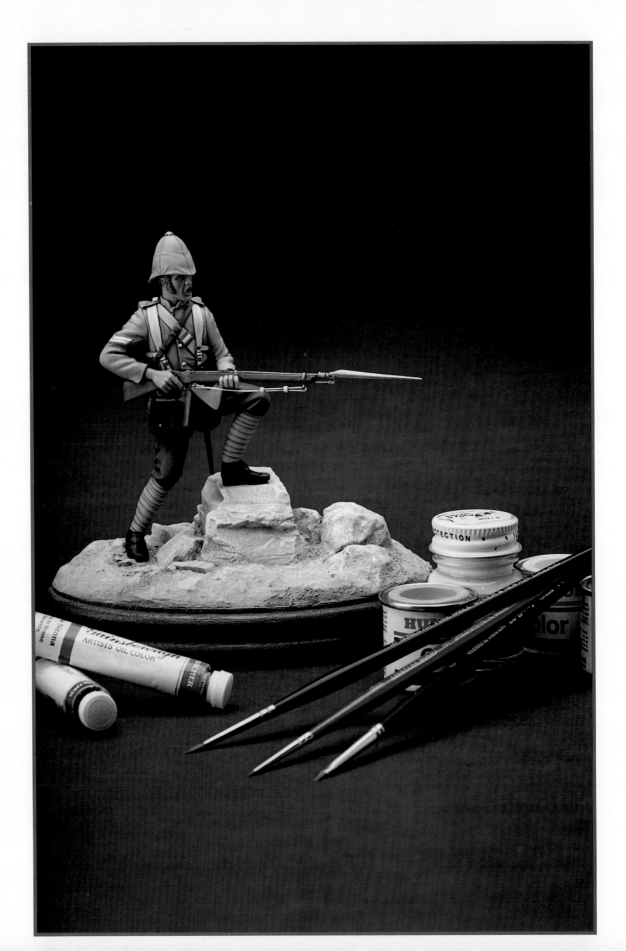

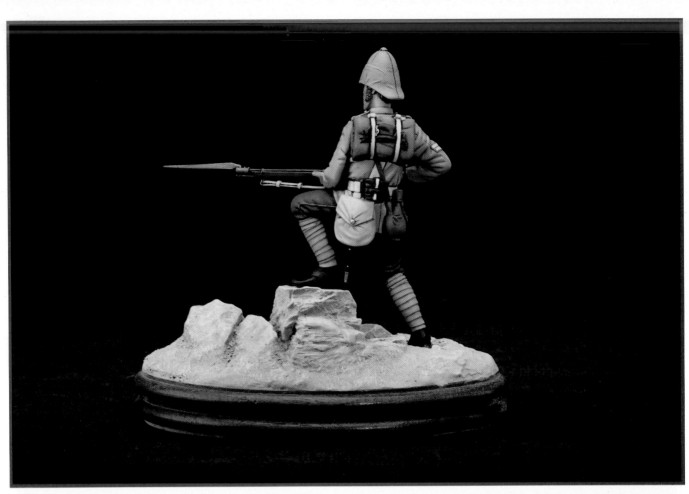

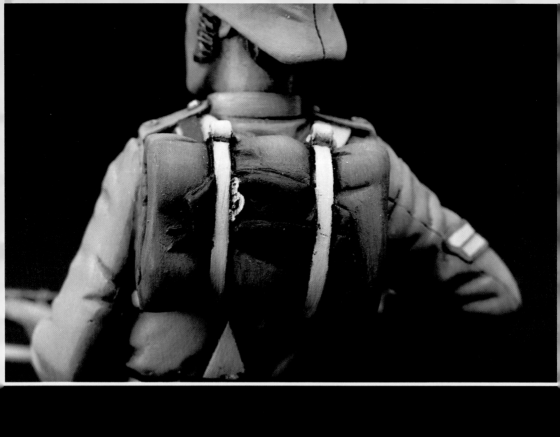

Gordon Highlander

British Infantry Officer

U. S. PILOT

MILITARY MINIATURE CLUBS

The Historical Miniature Society of Northeastern Oklahoma, 2214 E. 58th St., Tulsa, OK 74135

Military Miniature Society of Illinois, P.O. Box 394, Skokie, IL 60077

Southern California Area Miniature Modeler's Society, 11456 Broadmead, South El Monte, CA 91733

The Atlanta Soldier Society, 5168 Stratham Drive, Dunwoody, GA

Miniature Figure Collectors of America, 19 Mars Road, North Star, Newark, DE 19711

The Long Island Historical Miniature Collectors Society, P.O. Box 118, Wantagh, NY 11793

The Military Collectors of New England, P.O. Box 57076, Babson, MA 02157

National Capitol Model Soldier Society, 14613 Stonehouse Court, Silver Spring, MD 20905

Manitoba Model Soldier Society, 14 Thornewood Ave., Winnepeg, Manitoba, Canada, R2N 1K5

Ontario Model Soldier Society, 1176 Meander Ct., Mississauga, Ontario, Canada, L4Y 4A8

The Ottawa Valley Military Miniature Society, P.O. Box 9415, Terminal Ottawa, Ontario, Canada, K1G 3V1